"I want to let you know that something that I have been searching (and missing) for a long time: COURAGE." -*(Ellen) university professor*

"Reading *Fired Up Student Leadership* and attending class have changed my life. Before my college experience, I did not expect much from myself. Now, I understand that it is because one of the five domains was undiscovered. I had no passion….. Now, I do. I started believing in myself. I gained confidence. It took just one person. Believe in yourself or no one else will." - (Leslie) *Dr. R.'s former university student*

"I am in my chosen career because I followed my passion. That is when I found my purpose. I still use the same leadership concepts that Dr. R. taught us over twenty years ago." - *Dr. Rudnesky's former middle school student*

"When Frank became our principal, he recognized that no one person could do it all, and he went to work building teams and encouraging staff to explore their passions. Strong teams share strengths, they collaborate and celebrate to make things happen. I have always admired the way he encouraged leadership at all levels. With this philosophy, we all achieve!" -*Former Colleague*

Fired Up Student Leadership

Copyright © by Dr. Frank Rudnesky

ISBN 9798336262599

1st edition 2024

All rights reserved.

Nothing in this book may be reproduced in any form without written permission from the author.

Edited by Franki Maria Rudnesky.

Franki Maria Rudnesky is a writer currently working for an online news publication in Philadelphia. She earned her undergraduate degree from Saint Joseph's University, and received her Masters degree from Villanova University. Throughout her career, Franki has explored some of her many passions by working in journalism, social media, and education. She can be reached at fmrudnesky@gmail.com or on social media @frankirudnesky (Instagram), @frak.attack (TikTok), and @wordsbyfranki (X).

Cover art by Julie Gaupp (Jules)

Jules also works in the food and beverage industry but has always followed her passion for art because it fuels her soul and makes her heart smile. Her business, Jules Jewels, is ocean and surf inspired. She can often be seen at art shows and open-air markets at the Jersey Shore. You can reach her by email, purplecomet55@icloud.com or Instagram, @JulesJewels55 .

About the Author, Dr. Frank Rudnesky:

In addition to teaching at the high school and university levels, Dr. Frank Rudnesky was the principal of Belhaven Middle School in Linwood, New Jersey. During that time, the school was recognized with numerous local, state, and national awards for leadership, technology influence, excellence in performance, and a positive school culture. His school was often used as a visitation site for other educators from as far away as Japan, and they were the subject of a Japanese film documentary.

Dr. Rudnesky draws on his experience as an accomplished teacher, award-winning middle school principal, and transformational leader to deliver his captivating keynotes, workshops, and presentations to hundreds of audiences. As you listen to Dr. R.'s style of storytelling and his unconventional journey in life, it will get you *"Fired Up"* to pursue your passion and empower others to find their passion. His engagement, enthusiasm, and positive energy are contagious.

Dr. R. has developed, implemented, and studied leadership processes to enhance organizational behavior. He is the author of *Fired Up Leadership, Fired Up Teachership,* and *50 Great Things Leaders Do: Let's Get Fired Up* along with numerous articles published in the areas of leadership and technology influence. Dr. Rudnesky resides in the Jostens Renaissance Educator Hall of Fame and resided on several non-profit boards.

The author's humble background growing up has given him the foundation for life, leadership, and work ethic.

You can contact Dr. R. for keynotes, workshops, leadership camps, summits, academies, coaching, and professional development by email: FrankRudnesky@mail.com, or X and Instagram @DrFrankRud

Build Relationships — Sometimes you need to step out of your comfort zone. Keep building!

This book is dedicated to all of the educators in the arena, the people in our schools every day, paving the road to our future. Keep inspiring the next generation of leaders! Thank you!

Pictured above are EDU- rock stars from Henderson County High School (Conner & Ginger). They represent all of us!

Fired Up Student Leadership

Contents

Introduction..4

Leadership Styles 8

Domain One – Self-Management /Organization 11

Domain Two – Communication /Listening 25

Domain Three – Critical Thinking, Problem Solving, & Team Building....36

Domain Four – Character/Service 49

Domain Five – Passion 61

Conclusion 70

Appendix A Fired Up Leadership Design for Students 73

Appendix B – Fun Ideas 78

Appendix C -Gratitude Journal 83

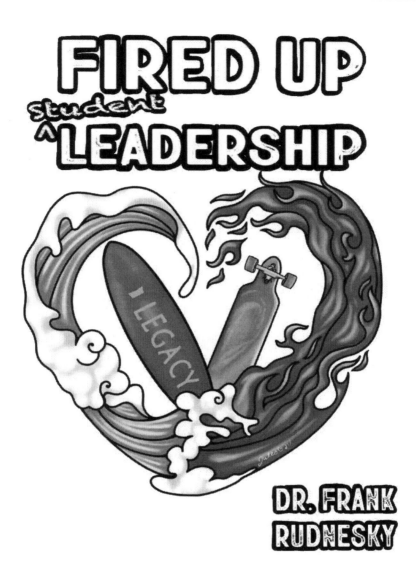

Get Fired Up, people!

Your mission and positivity may scare some people.

Scare some people anyway!

Fired Up Student Leadership:

Your guide to empower student leaders and transform your school into a Leadership School

This book is designed for educators and students.

Introduction

Start every day with love and gratitude.

Make it intentional.

See what happens.

People with more love and gratitude are happier. Happy people outperform unhappy people. That happiness becomes contagious and spreads to the people around you. When you understand and accept leadership opportunities, your life becomes better.

There should never be a cap on the number of leaders we create or the limits we place on ourselves. This book defines leadership using the Five Domains of *Fired Up Leadership,* and it creates your lifebook that flips the traditional model of leadership and sends you on a trajectory towards a growth mindset. Instead of making up versions of leadership in our minds that are lackluster, this book connects the dots and creates a true picture of leadership, validating the true meaning of your life's potential.

If I can be that conduit to a better life, a determination, or the right reason, then my leadership ability increases exponentially. Part of my mission is to strike a spark for other people as they start to discover their true abilities. The Five Domains of *Fired Up Leadership* was developed over decades of classroom instruction, research, camps, summits, institutes, academies, and collaborating with educators all over the world. I've seen beginnings, and I've seen outcomes. *Fired Up Leadership* works! Let's Go! Your leadership potential is about to be unleashed.

> *"Culture eats strategy for breakfast."*
>
> ## -attributed to Peter Drucker

The recipe for successful leadership includes many ingredients that should be continually fine-tuned. There are common threads that all high-performing schools have. Schools with a positive climate and culture outperform other schools significantly. Leadership has a major impact on climate and culture.

When one student looks in the mirror and sees themselves differently, a shift happens. A tipping point occurs. Not only do they see who they are, but they see who they can become. If you do not see yourself as a leader, you never truly become one. Change your perception; change your reality. Perception is reality.

Leadership is not a position. Leadership is not popularity. **Leadership is a choice.** It's one you will have to make every day. Unconditional love and unconditional leadership are a lot alike. And without love there is no leadership. If you treat love and leadership like verbs instead of just nouns and feelings, then amazing things start happening. You can raise the bar, set goals, never ask anyone to do something you would not do, lead by example, create a team, have integrity, think outside the box, treat people better than you want to be treated, and have fun! (*from 50 Great Things Leaders Do: Let's Get Fired Up! 2nd Edition, Rudnesky 2017)*

Think about Leadership as making yourself better so you can make the people around you better. Leaders will rise in many forms and include many traits. The qualities you already control will be some of your most powerful tools. These same qualities will contribute to the positive culture of your school. In other words, you will become an influencer, and you will help create a leadership school with like-minded people. "Building relationships" is your biggest asset!

"Thank you for changing my life from an ordinary kid to a leader. You have given us more leadership training than most adults." -Kurt (7th grader)

The above quote is from a then seventh-grade boy during an assembly to honor a leadership award our school just received. He was asked to speak a few words, and I had no idea what he was going to say. What he said confirmed the importance of student voice and the validity of giving every student multiple opportunities for leadership.

Life's challenges await us at every turn. These encounters create peaks and valleys that include failures and successes. When you start to challenge yourself in all areas of your life, you will begin to find out everything you need to know about leadership. Commitment will be a key component to balance your life. For instance, do not be afraid to try out for a team, a stage play, or join a club. You never know how it might turn out. Go for a jog, walk on the beach, or take a class that might challenge you.

Over my career as an educator, dozens of students have told me that they were not smart, talented, or able. Those statements reminded me of moments in my own past when I thought I was unintelligent, untalented, or incapable. Because some students viewed themselves in a negative light, my leadership paradigm shifted. It enabled me to see situations from a better student "point of view." In turn, my leadership parameters expanded to include more people. When your limits get bigger, it creates a path for more people to get involved.

> ***Create a place where everyone wants to be, and incredible results can be achieved.***

Leadership Styles

Fired Up Leadership is based on two different leadership styles: transformational leadership and servant leadership. Transformational leaders focus on the people in the organization, inspiring them to reach their potential by creating leadership opportunities for everyone. Where transformational leadership is promoted, people are challenged to reach their full potential by being aligned with tasks that are meaningful.

Meaningless tasks do not engage people over time. When people begin to feel unimportant, they become disengaged, and negativity becomes more prominent. Because we naturally want to make a positive difference, we need to be challenged and included. When we engage, challenge, and include, a positive climate and culture are the result. The positives become so loud that the negativity becomes mute. Toxic team members become irrelevant.

> **The biggest form of identity theft is telling someone they can't accomplish something.**

Servant leadership is similar to transformational leadership because your organizational success depends on the attention you devote to your colleagues and community. Service is a key component and one of the five domains of *Fired Up Leadership*. Serve before you lead.

Servant leadership plus transformational leadership equals resultant leadership. That is where *Fired Up Leadership* is born. Resultant leaders are always creating opportunities for more people to become leaders. This generates a combined effect that initiates a "pay it forward" mentality involving shared values, beliefs, and behaviors.

Below, Figure 1 illustrates the Five Domains of *Fired Up Leadership.* All the domains are equally important, and they feed one another. You do not have to do them sequentially, but you will do them simultaneously. At the center of the leadership model is your passion. It's what drives you, and it leads to your purpose.

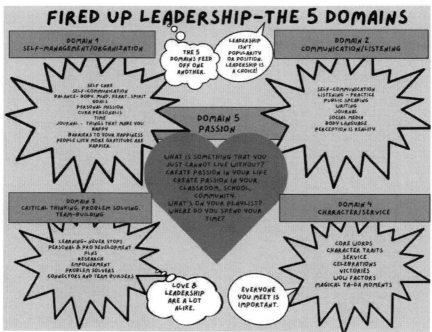

Figure 1 – The Five Domains of Fired Up Leadership

Fired Up Student Leadership

Domain One: Self-Management/Organization

"Expect a lot from yourself or no one else will."

Everything starts with you. Self-Management/Organization can be the most effective component to life and leadership. It can also be a major barrier to your success at every level. When you continually fine-tune the quality of your life, amazing accomplishments are always within reach.

These concepts work with people of all ages. The following is an excerpt from a university leadership class student: *"While reading Fired Up Leadership, my mindset and attitude towards life as a whole changed. I realized that by challenging myself to be the best I can be, staying positive, and starting each day with love, gratitude, and self-care that I can achieve anything I put my mind to."*

Self-care is not a fad. Self-care is action, and healthy habits take a commitment. If you approach any of the five domains as a quick fix, then you will be disappointed. You may be successful in the short-term, but no long-term gain is possible. Self-care becomes a strong part of your life and your leadership style.

Becoming and staying healthier should be a part of your personal mission. Self-care turns on the light, helps you stay balanced, and clears the path to your EPIC: Where your Exceptional talents meet your Passion guided by your Intelligence and Character, therein lies your EPIC.

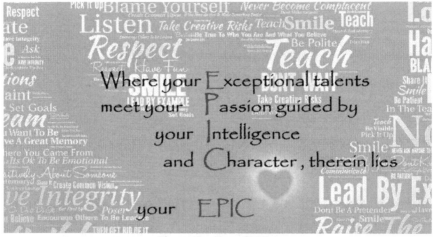

Figure 2 – Your EPIC

Some strategies to organize your life are really simple like packing a healthy lunch the night before school and making your bed before you leave in the morning. No matter what your day looks like, you will come home to some form of organization: You had a healthy meal, a neat bed, and a personal victory. Keep your room clean. Organize your academic classes. Ask adults you trust for help. Use a planning calendar.

Another simple concept: Clean up after yourself. A little time now saves a lot of time later. Literally, how long does it take to clean a toilet? More than half of the students I ask do not know because they have never done it. The same with every footprint you leave wherever you go. Start those easy self-care habits as early as possible. Believe it or not, it's a road to your Domain One independence: Self-Management/Organization.

Hygiene also needs to be mentioned. I am not going over everything you need to do but have a routine. It adds to a healthier you. Look healthy. Feel healthy. Be healthy.

As your life becomes organized, start writing down your goals. In the broadest form of a statement, anytime you want to do something, you should do it; accomplish it. But you need to start with a focus. Remarkable things can be achieved when we eliminate common barriers of insignificance, lack of time management, and an absence of commitment.

Start self-communicating the positives. Self-communication becomes another habit. It happens when you repeatedly tell yourself what you can accomplish and then put together your goals and plan of action. Make it a part of your routine. Some contemporary authors call this self-talk or self-affirmations. You will read more about self-communication in Domain Two.

This book has many blank spaces for you to write down ideas. Please feel free to create an online document to access your thoughts and progress from anywhere. This book consists of about ten thousand words that the author (me) wrote. This book will also consist of thousands of words that you write. Congratulations! You are about to get *Fired Up!* As previously mentioned, "Happy people outperform unhappy people."

How do I get to that happy place?

As fast as you can:

Write down five (or more) things that make you happy:

_____

_____

_____

_____

_____

Now spend time doing those things.

Happy people are generally more sociable, flexible, and accepting. There is a strong connection between gratitude and happiness. Be intentional with your gratitude. Your actions will reflect your intentions. There is a place in the back of this book

(Appendix C) to continue a Gratitude Journal. Use it! Make it your own. Be grateful for what you have and what you will have. Write down three GREAT things about you that you want people to know: (For example, I would write: I am a girl dad. I like to smile, and I am a magician.)

1 _____

2 _____

3 _____

Chances are that these three great things will turn out to be things that make you happy.

In the space below, write down three GREAT things about your school:

1 _____

2 _____

3 _____

Now write down three GREAT things you want your school to do:

1 _____

2 _____

3 _____

The chances of you accomplishing your goals increase significantly when you write them down. You should approach teaching and learning from a "whole person" perspective. In other words, stay balanced in all four areas of you: Body, Mind, Heart, and Spirit. If you spend all your time on your mind and never exercise the other areas, over time you will feel out of whack. You will never reach your full potential. This is an example of balanced goals for the week that I would write for myself:

Body- Exercise five days per week- Monday (8 am), Tuesday (8 am), Wednesday (8 am), Friday (8 am), Saturday (9 am)

Mind- Read at least twenty minutes per day, write at least twenty minutes per day, research twice or more per week

Heart – Promote leadership on social media. Practice magic four days per week. Family time: dinner, programs, activities

Spirit – Mindfulness every day. Skateboard or run at least once per week. Wake up each day with love and gratitude. Listen to music and dance like no one is looking. Produce inspirational videos: *Fired Up Fridays with Frank!*

Now you try it. Write down goals for the next week in all areas of you:

_____

_____

_____

_____

_____

Most people do not write or schedule goals for mental health. Just like we all have periods of physical illness, we all have times of mental illness. Sometimes we have a cold and sometimes it's more severe like the flu or a virus. Most of it is not severe.

Sometimes we need to practice breathing to calm our minds and sometimes we need to seek a more clinical approach. Be proactive in your approach to all areas of your health. Recently, people have placed more emphasis on mental health awareness and social-emotional teaching and learning. If you cannot think of any ways to become healthier mentally, ask an adult you trust and look back at your goals. Spend time in your happy places and with people you enjoy. There are also many "mindfulness" videos online. Try it! It takes about three minutes.

A friend of mine, Shilpi Mahajan, has some amazing videos on YouTube. Here is a link to one of her mindfulness videos: https://www.youtube.com/watch?v=ihwcw_ofuME&t=58s

Or

If you practiced goal setting before you read this book, you may have been introduced to SMART goal setting. There is a plethora of information online including downloadable worksheets that you may want to use. To put it briefly, make your goals: Specific, Measurable, Achievable, Relevant, and Time-bound.

You should also set goals in different areas of your life. Just as balance in your body is important, balance in your life is equally important. Balance your home, work, school, social life, hobbies, and passion.

Your goals can change from week to week. That is not uncommon. Examine your accomplishments and adjust your plan. Reflect. Long-term goals will take more planning and reflection. Your short-term goals will take planning, too.
Most of your life has been set up for you. In high school, you know what time you arrive, leave, practice, meet, and eat. When you hit college, trade school, or the work world, time

management becomes a more essential component in all areas of your life's success. Time can be your friend or your enemy.

Use a calendar to schedule your most important events around external forces. These events are what is most important to your happiness and accomplishing your goals. If you do not have a calendar, start one. You can print one out or keep it online.

You know when you work, sleep, practice, have mandatory meetings, etc. Schedule your exercise, meal preparation, mindfulness, yoga, art, family time, and whatever is most important to you. As much as possible, keep your calendar on schedule. This tip will keep you on a positive path. We plan medical appointments, so why not plan our workouts, too?

Now, you can regulate your positive choices and outcomes. In the simplest explanation, you can control your attitude and your ability to achieve most goals. Although the time in a day is finite, each morning brings about a new set of hours.

> ### *86,400 – 1,440 – 24 – 1*
>
> ### *What are you going to do with it?*

Try combining happiness with your goals. It's a life changer.

These are some of mine:

Read more for enjoyment. Go to the beach more. Watch the sunrise at the beach. Skateboard on the boardwalk more. Listen to five favorite songs every day. Ask people I love to share their favorite songs with me. Express my gratitude more. Share my kindness. Drink more water. Try a new recipe. Treat myself with dignity every day. Talk to someone I would never talk to. Call my oldest living relative. Be a better listener. Do something my wife wants to do. Go to more concerts. Go to a ball game. Hike a national park. Go boating. Hold up inspirational signs. Go to a Broadway show. Give service. Set better examples. Play music in front of my class. Look for good in people. Play basketball more. Play wiffle ball. Step outside my comfort zone. Get hired to speak at fifty schools. Be present. Prioritize what matters most. Stand up for my beliefs. Attack my daily goals. Enjoy my creativity. Paint my masterpiece.

Personal Mission Statement

Your personal mission requires a deep and continual reflection about who you are and the positive messages you send to the people around you. My mission statement is, "Continually fine-tune the quality of my life and the lives of the people around me through commitment and hard work while having fun."

Your mission statement should start out as pages of reflection. I want my mission to define my legacy. Start creating your personal mission statement. Keep this book handy to review and refine it over time. There is no right or wrong definition of who you are, but also keep in mind who you want to be. Your mission should be in line with your long-term life goals. Your life is a work in progress.

Things to think about and write down:

What character traits and leadership qualities do I want to display and pass on?

Who are your role models? Why?

What leadership qualities do they display? What traits do you want to display?

What unique contributions can you make to the world and the people around you?

Character Traits _____

_____

Leadership Qualities _____
_____
_____

Role Models (These are people that have made a positive impact on you, your champions.) _____
_____
_____
_____

Famous Quotes _____
_____
_____

Draft _____
_____
_____
_____
_____

_____

_____

_____

_____

_____

What are your favorite points from Domain One? Read them out loud to someone.

_____

_____

_____

_____

_____

_____

_____

On the last day of every month on your calendar write: Am I where I want to be?

- ➤ **Domain One: Self-Management/Organization**
    - o Practice self-care in all areas: Body, Mind, Heart, & Spirit
        - Daily hygiene

- Schedule priorities
- Organize your calendar/manage time
  - Be able to work independently
  - Assume responsibility
- Keep a gratitude journal
- Set short term and long-term goals and be able to effectively carry the plan to achieve these goals.
  - Write goals for each week and marking period
  - Write goals for each year
  - Develop a personal mission statement
- Be able to define and understand Leadership Styles.
  - Servant Leadership
  - Transformational Leadership
  - Resultant Leadership
- Effectively manage your attitude.

Fired Up Student Leadership

Domain Two: Communication/Listening

"Leadership is communicating to people their worth and potential so clearly that they come to see it in themselves."
-Stephen R. Covey

Creating more leaders is part of my mission. If I can bridge that gap and open minds for people to see themselves differently, then the status quo is challenged in a positive way. One of the keys to making this happen is self-communication.

Self-Communication

In the simplest form of a definition, self-communication is communicating with yourself. When we say it out loud, it may feel silly but we really need to tell ourselves what we are capable of accomplishing. No matter what our barriers are, there is no ceiling on our achievements. If you think you can, then you can.

High expectations rub off on the people around you. You must first communicate this to yourself before you can pass on the theory to other people in your school. Your self-communication becomes part of your daily communication with the people around you.

When you put your mind to it, your positive thoughts can allow your body to overcome many barriers. These accomplishments may take hard work and commitment, but it all starts with a positive mindset and confidence in yourself. Self-communication creates assurance and powerful results.

Have you ever witnessed someone gossiping when a person leaves the room? How did you react? Here's a great idea: Hang out with people that talk positively about other people when they leave the room. Be the person that throws out compliments like confetti in the absence of those people.

Try this positive self-communication:

Say this out loud!

I am smart.

I am strong.

I am beautiful.

I am kind.

I am loved.

I am AMAZING!

Now, act accordingly.

> *Motivate yourself, inspire others.*

Gratitude

People with more gratitude are happier. Happy people outperform unhappy people. Communicate your gratitude. Gratitude is one component of happiness we can all bring to the rest of the world once we decide to live that *Fired Up* life. Once you commit, it's a constant ride to improve yourself and the people around you. When people know you appreciate and love them, they are more accountable and responsible.

As quickly as possible, list the things you are grateful for:

_____

_____

_____

_____

Make sure you start or continue your gratitude journal that is in the back of this book. Add to it every week or every day. My short gratitude list for this week includes: Family, friends, students, speeches, professional development, pets, school visits, exercise, reading, writing, and music.

Other ways to be intentionally grateful are to reach out to people in a variety of ways: writing thank you notes, talking to people you would never talk to, politeness, kindness, smiling more, hold the door for someone, and thanking the people that wait on you – cashiers, attendants, servers, etc. Make it intentional and make it a part of your daily journey.

Attitude

Gratitude translates into a positive attitude, and/or positive attitude renders gratitude. You have total control over two things every day: your responses and your attitude. It starts as soon as you wake up. When your feet hit the floor, start your day with gratitude. Some people let the slightest thing set them off in a negative direction. Who are you going to be today? Control your destiny or someone else will, and you might not like the outcome. Your positive attitude will be an asset to your leadership style. When you have barriers and conflict use them as opportunities to improve the quality of your leadership. It's not always easy but it will allow you and the people around you to be more successful in the long-run.

People who are negative, underachieving, and complainers contribute to a toxic environment. Conversely, your positive attitude becomes contagious. For instance, always use compliments as part of your demeanor but make it sincere: "Wow, your hair looks great!" "I love your shoes." "Thank you for being here!" Focus on the positives, and you will find them. Fuel their fire and the people around you discover their beauty!

Name ways to show gratitude and allow people to feel important:

_____

_____

_____

_____

Listening

We communicate in many different ways, both verbally and nonverbally. We read, write, talk, listen, and observe body language. Listening can become one of your biggest relationship builders. In the book *The 7 Habits of Highly Effective People*, author Stephen R. Covey illustrates how to truly become an empathetic listener by describing five levels of listening. They include ignoring, pretend listening, selective listening, attentive listening, and empathic listening.

What do you think each means? Discuss it with a friend. Have a group discussion.

Most people want to talk more than they want to listen. Even quiet people are not always great listeners. Sometimes, people will interpret their conversation with you as what they want to hear. They will interpret your conversation with how they relate to the topic. Most people interpret a conversation selectively. They do not hear what you are actually saying.

To become a great listener, you must practice. It's like any other area in our lives where we choose to go beyond proficiency. Practice listening to other people, and actually try to interpret what they are saying. If you do not fully understand, ask. Listen intentionally. Some of the worst listening techniques are cutting people off, raising your voice, and not trying to understand how the person feels.

Can you think of times when you were a bad listener? Think about it then write down how you could have changed your listening habits:

_____

_____

_____

_____

_____

Public Speaking

Another important component of communication is public speaking. As leaders, we must create these public speaking opportunities. These chances can occur in a variety of settings, mostly by doing it. In a school, you can build it into any curriculum, club meetings, presentations, idea exchanges, and research. Because people may not create these opportunities on their own, we must lead them to these opportunities so that they become habits. Lead by example.

Name some ways to create public speaking opportunities:

_____

_____

_____

_____

_____

_____

_____

Social Media

The possibilities that technology brings to communication absolutely thrills and scares me at the same time. Your communication will always include the backdrop that the world provides, and smartphones have quickly taken over the information overload. Communication through technology happens so fast and it can go viral in minutes, which makes it both advantageous and threatening at home, school, and work. The most popular form of communication for people under fifty is texting, and the gap keeps increasing.

It's highly important to infuse positive character traits into tech communication. Many people feel masked by social media to the point of anonymity, but you should always think about all potential ramifications before you act online. As adults, we must self-communicate the importance of integrity with social media and allow our modeling to pave the positive way for other students and colleagues.

Name ways to practice good character traits on social media:

_____

_____

_____

Body Language

Body language can be tricky. Many times, it is misread. Because I am an educator, speaker, facilitator, and author, I am in front of many people almost every day. Also, just like you, I frequently communicate with friends and family using body language.

I pick up signals because I look for them. The most important way to interpret body language may be to ask a person a question. You would be surprised at the answers you get. In other words, just like all communication, it requires practice. You can make a game of it with friends or family by taking turns using body language and trying to guess what the other person is portraying, similar to the old game of charades. If you do not know what that game is, ask the oldest person you know. Basically, it is making up gestures and talking without speaking.

What do think are the top five to ten takeaways from Domain Two? Another task is to teach a section of D2.

How will you practice these takeaways?

_____

_____

_____

_____

_____

- ➢ **Domain Two: Communication/Listening**
    - Use a variety of written, oral, digital, and nonverbal communication to articulate and develop leadership skills
        - Become an effective listener through authentic listening habits
            - Practice
            - Use team builders and connectors
        - Improve public speaking skills
            - Infused in curriculum and/or workshops
            - Develop a digital portfolio
            - Develop competency in digital communication
                - Podcasting
                - Video - casting
            - Read out loud and make presentations to elementary

schools, senior citizens, and at conferences
- Write a variety of essays
  - Infused into the curriculum using a variety of character & service topics
  - Writing prompts & free writing journal entries
- Deliver information properly and timely

Fired Up Student Leadership

Domain Three: Critical Thinking, Problem-Solving, and Team-Building

"We are definitely better together."

Domain Three may give you the competitive edge that separates you from other classmates, leaders, and career seekers. Your ability to think critically, solve problems, and contribute as a team member will definitely be some of your most valuable assets that create success in anything you do. Likewise, people will look to you as a contributor to their success as you create synergy in these areas.

Critical Thinking

As students and leaders, we continually look for better ways of teaching and learning to allow ourselves and colleagues to reach, and then expand, our potential. When we stop learning, we stop leading. Effective leaders are constantly educating themselves and the people around them. We are in search of knowledge. We frequently review the literature, take classes, teach, attend conferences, facilitate sessions, and learn from each other. One of your main components of leadership in

Domain Three is to be able to facilitate learning for other students and teachers. As you facilitate, you become more proficient yourself.

In addition to using some traditional methods, you will learn to differentiate your delivery of teaching and learning. In other words, use the people around you to help you learn and appeal to the "whole person." Similarly, the people you associate with create a knowledge base that you do not have. Their experiences and training will greatly increase ideas that allow you to think differently, unconventionally, and from a new perspective. More ideas create more options. Keep bringing non-traditional thinkers to the leadership arena. People are unique in some ways and alike in so many others. Your experiences, learning, and teaching styles are just as important as published research because you begin to do your own action research.

Relationship building becomes part of your critical thinking. It allows you to find the strengths of the people around you. In turn, those same people will find your strengths. Together, we make each other better. Then you can maximize your leadership success.

We all have a plethora of knowledge at the end of our fingertips. I mean this literally. You can look anything up on your smartphone and then disseminate that information to your entire organization seamlessly. Just make sure it is legitimate. Sometimes it helps significantly to triangulate your data (use several sources) to make an informed decision. I think that is where a lot of people get hung up. They rely on partial information.

If you really want to learn a lot about life, observe children. They (we) are born without boundaries, and they offer terrific insight. Instead of telling you what you want to hear, they tell you the truth. The truth always works in the long run even if there are consequences to your opinion. Only after children are influenced by adults do they become less free about their opinions. This is when their bias begins. Never stifle the creativity of our youth. Sometimes, we may even need to think like a child, and have no boundaries. At the other end of the age spectrum, talk to the oldest people you know. They are living history and love to talk.

As fast as you can, write down five things about anything you want to learn:

_____

_____

_____

Write down ways you can learn them:

Who are your oldest living relatives?

Talk to them. What did they have to say? Report back.

Problem-Solving

The first step in problem-solving is to identify the problem. After you identify the problem, eliminate yourself as a barrier. For instance, some people have glitches because they create them in their own minds. They look at threats and weaknesses without considering the opportunities and strengths. When you look at all internal and external factors, consider every educated solution to the problem. With every conflict, there comes opportunity.

If you do have a problem, then you can proceed to ask yourself: Is the problem definitive? If it is, state the problem and do a SWOT analysis (strengths, weaknesses, opportunities, threats). List the strengths (inside your organization and you), and the weaknesses (inside your organization and you). Now you must list the opportunities (outside your organization and you), and the threats (outside your organization and you). Compare the two sides. What are your possible solutions? There should be more than one. Which one is the most feasible? Now come up with a plan. This plan will be important. Your strengths will be the team's strengths. The same is true with the rest of your team. Likewise, use your strengths to devour the weaknesses of your team. Your available resources and monetary situation will have an effect on your plan.

> ***The combined strengths of your team will eliminate team weaknesses to solve any problem.***

List a problem or potential barrier to increasing leadership opportunities for everyone, then solve it. Some opportunities for leadership include: Setting up events, facilitating events, recruiting class and school ambassadors, collaborating with other classes, visiting other schools, service projects, and collaborating with people you never met when you visit those other schools.

Identify the Problem: _____

_____

Strengths (internal): _____

_____

Weaknesses (internal): _____

_____

Opportunities (external): _____

_____

Threats (external): _____

_____

Possible Solutions: _____

_____

_____

_____

_____

Team Building

In all leadership training, we spend a lot of time in the team building area because it's productive, fun, and it strengthens all domains of *Fired Up Leadership*. Team building increases the performance of our schools and it helps to eliminate the weaknesses of our team members. By working together, we increase our overall performance to complete tasks, goals, and achievements.

Team building can be tricky for a number of reasons. There is an abundance of information out there on numerous media sites. My favorites are Pinterest and YouTube. A lot of information is free and relevant. Also, understand that a large number of activities can be cliché and overrated but those same activities are well received in some forums. In other words: "Know your audience."

Also, "Know your delivery point." Everything you do may not appeal to your entire audience or every participant but you can gear your activities to appeal to the majority. Know your goals for the meeting, day, month, and year. What are you trying to accomplish? Trust and collegiality are two components of successful team-building. If at all possible, when you are planning for your entire team, department, or leadership group, take them off site or out of the classroom as a bonding experience and to try something new.

Accumulate your own action research about what worked during certain situations and fine-tune the process. Accentuate new beginnings with team building. For instance, start your new year or new project with a team building field trip. Create a renaissance. Announce a new theme and service-learning platform then dig right in. If you go to an offsite location, have a scavenger hunt or go to a place of service. Food is always good, and you don't need a hefty budget.

This is an example of a themed team building day:

One year, we had inclement weather so we had to do everything onsite but we kept it moving. The guest speaker we scheduled couldn't make it either. Be prepared. This is an example of an onsite retreat: First, we introduced our new theme "School Rocks!" Then we had a video conference with our guest speaker to announce our service learning: renewable energy. We proceeded with a short meeting to do some housekeeping and raise our level of awareness. This particular year, we created a stimulating video to jumpstart our day. We included as many recent pictures of our building and people that we could find. We promoted our goals then tied it to the Olympics that just ended. It was easy to find encouragement in some of the

Olympic pictures and connect the visuals to hard work, commitment, and "whatever it takes."

Later in the day, people were ready to eat and replenish their bodies as well as spirits. Be sensitive to any allergies and beliefs. We let people know in advance what we were making. It was nice to communicate on a level that didn't involve mostly work related jargon.

The room should be filled with laughter and anticipation. For another team building activity, we divided our large group into different "rock groups." Each participant got a "backstage pass" with a number on the back; this designated their team for the day. Now we had teams for our competition/team building. We used a big dry erase board in the front of the room for a visual and to keep score. The first task was to name your "rock group." It was hilarious and interesting as each group sent a representative onstage to announce the names. The next task was to brainstorm ideas for our service project. The teams wrote the ideas on big paper and taped it to the wall. We put a time limit on this to keep it moving. After time was called, each group read their ideas. We then moved to the gymnasium. We had music set up to greet everyone.

First up was the "Rock Star Relay." Each group (band) competed against each other dressing up, running to mid-court then tagging the next person to do the same. There were many photo opportunities during this one. We finished the competition with "Name That Tune." We had several categories. Each team had a representative. The facilitator played a tune until someone guessed it. We went back to the auditorium and tallied the points.

Our closing ceremony was complete with an Olympic-style medal ceremony and the national anthem. We debriefed and tied everything together. It's funny how some people remembered working in a place that wasn't fun. Granted, I can guarantee you that some people were not as enthusiastic as I was, but for the most part, everyone felt appreciated, connected, and inspired! Flexibility played a big part in the day but we were prepared. It worked. Some activities became traditions. You must fine-tune them every year.

Many of these activities can be done virtually. Use your imagination. Because of the recent pandemic, I get many questions about team building remotely. For instance, each team member can have a beach ball and pass it from screen to screen and words added virtually on social media with a unique hashtag. Be creative. You will be amazing.

Here are some recent team-building activities I used with all ages: https://www.youtube.com/watch?v=8PJSpLiCQvA

or

Never underestimate yourself or the people around you. On your first day of a new school year, celebrate with outright engagement of the entire facility. At the beginning of every school year, get everyone excited to return to the campus for a new beginning and a strong start. IT'S THE ONLY FIRST DAY YOU GET! Remember, in the previous section I described how our employees started their new year, now, the whole school celebrates. We did a lot of similar activities for the students that we did before the students started their school year.

Always begin with music, enthusiasm, and lots of smiles. Make everyone feel welcome. The last class to arrive in the auditorium was always our upperclassmen. We rolled out the red carpet and gave them a standing ovation. After the national anthem, we count in the new year. Since we had a rock theme that year, we struck a gong rather than drop a ball. It's similar to the New York City Times Square celebration on the traditional New Year. It's a great starting point.

When everyone in your school feels empowered, problem-solving and the team approach become proactive. People feel creative, important, and action oriented. Great thinkers become great doers. Action is a key for opening the doors to positive climate and culture as you continue to create a leadership school. At the end of the day, we take a team picture.

As fast as you can, write down the most important components of Domain Three. Then after reading the bulleted points take your time to discover how you will implement them both individually and as a group. Then teach a section to someone.

_____

_____

_____

_____

_____

_____

_____

_____

- **Domain Three: Critical Thinking, Problem Solving, & Team Building**
    - Consider different points of view.
    - Identify, analyze, and solve problems.
        - Use a SWOT Analysis
            - Strengths
            - Weaknesses
            - Opportunities
            - Threats
        - Create an action plan
    - Demonstrate teamwork skills.
        - Empower others
        - Travel with your school or other organizations
        - Learn from professionals outside of your school
        - Participate in a club, sport, band, and/or community organization
        - Complete a list of challenges
            - Participate in a Leadership Exchange with another school
                - Facilitate planning, learning, activities
                - Exchange ideas with other schools

Fired Up Student Leadership

Domain Four: Character/Service

"The only people to get even with are those that have helped you." -Anonymous

Character Traits

Just like leadership qualities are intertwined, so are character traits. As your confidence in your leadership ability grows, so does your positive personality. Affirmative character becomes intentional because it's a habit. Your positive character traits become your core values. They become aligned with your goals and mission. What is the first thing you think about in the morning?

> ***Part of leadership is becoming the best version of "you."***

As fast as you can, list your favorite character traits. Some of my other favorite character traits include kindness, gratitude, respect, passion, integrity, patience, compassion, empathy, trustworthiness, and strength.

_____

_____

_____

_____

_____

_____

_____

Look at the traits you wrote. Will leadership be effective without the presence of those traits? Chances are it will not be. Your positive character forges your leadership path. Any positive character that you use in your *Leadership Lifebook* will become an attribute to your leadership legacy. Remember, no one is perfect at character so when you make a mistake it's fine to apologize and then move on in a positive direction.

There are many character traits that will build your leadership repertoire. One example is kindness. Imagine if everyone had a goal of one intentional kind gesture each day. Your school would be different. The world would be different. Your school would be easily identified as a leadership school. Students become influencers.

We often gave public speaking opportunities to students during our leadership events. One year at our "Student Leadership Beach Bash," the keynote speaker was a fourteen-year-old that participated in our year long Leadership Academy. She spoke eloquently when she said:

"Today I am going to advocate for something I believe in. I believe in kindness and as cliché as that may sound, it is the truth. I don't know what my classmates struggle with or what their home lives are. Maybe school is an escape for them... Don't be the person that makes them feel embarrassed. It's easier to smile and give a compliment than it is to be degrading or hurtful. Just be kind...... we all struggle, we all fail. So, appreciate the voice you have. Advocate for something you believe in. Nothing changes if we sit here and wait. Hear me, I hear you. Just be kind."

The school where I worked as a principal is close to the beach. During our leadership training with other schools, I started to use a beach ball to demonstrate the connection of character and leadership. The "beach ball" became a staple of training wherever I went. We passed around the beach ball, and each person wrote a word that describes leadership then passes it to someone else. At the end of the session, I collect the ball and hold it up. I read some of the words and the connections are apparent.

Over the years, I accumulated over 10,000 words. According to students between the ages of ten and twenty-two, overwhelmingly, the number one quality of a leader is some form of positive character.

Ask people you know for a word that describes leadership. What did you come up with? Write them down:

_____

_____

_____

_____

_____

Do they compare to yours?

Service

The framework of leadership does not exist without service. Serve before you lead. Service can change the trajectory of your school and your community. Service allows people to have a voice. By having this mindset, the two become intertwined. You cannot have a leadership school that does not include service.

Now that you are on your way to mastering positive thinking, focus on the power of positive "doing." When you model positive behavior, and get your team involved, your influence and the influence of your organization will go beyond what you thought possible.

There is a difference between community service and service learning. Most people have never really thought about it because they may be pressured into piling up hours of service. Community service connects hours or some other resource to your community. There is no real learning or commitment taking place.

Service learning is actually making the connection to the community and discovering their needs. It is a proactive approach that creates awareness. Then you follow through on satisfying that need to make the community or group better. Service learning can also be described as community involvement: a connection for the betterment of people around you. Awareness is a key to systemic change.

Many student groups require community service hours without the notion of a plan to make a difference. There is nothing wrong with collecting hours as long as it satisfies the other needs of the school and/or community. Measure it differently. The planning part is important when formulating servant leadership. Service learning is an important component to the framework of the positive climate and culture of a school.

What are the needs of the organization or community?

What are your special talents and/or the talents of your group, club, or school that can aid these needs?

How can you be most effective?

Take a long look at how you can make yourself, the people around you, and your community better. There are many opportunities for your organization to get involved and make a difference locally and globally. Some are really simple, and they take minimal time and money. It can be as easy as talking to senior citizens, cleaning, or helping people with yard work. You might be surprised at how many people do not have the support of their families to get simple tasks accomplished.

One year our school raised money for an organization that brings clean water systems to Chinese orphanages. Another year we sponsored a cancer support organization in our community. Other years we supported local food banks and homeless shelters. There are many opportunities for service learning. Come up with a plan and execute it. Make it fun, like the year we skateboarded to collect new pairs of socks for the homeless.

Honk if you love someone - Acts of character and service intertwine as your leadership skills progress. They become commonplace. Someone sent me a link to this video on YouTube. They said it was "all me" meaning it was something that fit into our school. Check out the video. It is about one man's mission to bring happiness to the people around him and send them in a positive trajectory.

https://www.youtube.com/watch?v=1EwYLZmkUxo

Or

It proves just how easy it can be to put a smile on someone's face, change their day, give service, and promote positive leadership. I felt compelled to try it out at our middle school. So, I did! I used it with my advisory group, at Leadership Camp, and it became a staple of my everyday greetings for the students and parents.

With my students, we watched the aforementioned video and then replicated the project in front of our school. My face still hurts from laughing and smiling so much. We made designs similar to the ones in the video, *Honk if you love someone, Honk if you are happy, You are awesome, Have a beautiful day.* I also made a permanent sign to put on our sidewalk. The students were completely invested and engaged. Cars, vans, and trucks were honking and smiling.

Welcome Sign Wednesday – Unbeknownst to me, a friend that is a principal in Massachusetts @DrCSJones, began holding up signs on Wednesdays with his students. (Thank you, Dr. Jones!) He calls it: "Welcome Sign Wednesdays." I was inspired by his version and started spreading the word in all the schools I visited. They all came up with their own versions. I do it in front of my university classes and the schools I visit for leadership training, keynotes, and professional development.

When your mind is set on making a positive difference, service-learning opportunities will arise. Service contributes to a life of leadership. Put a plan in place, and your role will be obvious as your compass points in the right direction of "true north leadership." You will see the needle on your leadership compass shift in a positive direction. Although your school or organization may plan a service project, sometimes the world around you may alter your plans. As your leadership ability progresses, so does your ability to adapt to unexpected occurrences. Your adaptability becomes another part of your leadership repertoire.

Although your school or clubs within your school may have service platforms, you can also "pay it forward" with your own. What personal service projects can you think of to provide by yourself? An example may be helping an elderly neighbor or reading to younger children.

In the space below, name and describe a personal project.

_____

_____

_____

_____

_____

_____

_____

_____

_____

_____

_____

Summarize Domain Four and then read it out loud to someone and teach it to someone.

- **Domain Four – Character/Service**
  - Demonstrate character traits.
    - Each month, a different character trait (leadership quality) is applied across the curriculum
    - A variety of ideas are shared on digital media
    - Students will announce the traits in audio, video, and print
  - Complete service learning.
    - Read to senior citizens and/or children
    - Facilitate your own community service project – "Pay It Forward"
    - Complete service at a food bank, homeless shelter, assisted living center, etc.

Fired Up Student Leadership

Domain Five: Passion

"Follow your passion, and you will find your purpose."

We need more fire! A leadership culture builds healthy relationships and creates a culture of passion. A movement of creativity is sparked. Teachers become facilitators and students become inventors, writers, artists, pioneers, and scientists rather than passive learners. People are permitted to go places they never thought possible.

At different points in your life, your inner light may dim, but then someone appears and shows you the endless possibilities you bring to the world. It becomes reciprocal. You want to bring that fire to other people. Your environment becomes an infectious realm of positivity.

Passion comes from the heart and it manifests itself in emotion, enthusiasm, commitment, and a path to your purpose. Some people never find it, or they are afraid to pursue it. Your passion guides you because it brings you joy. Along the journey, your human capacity grows in all of your dimensions: body, mind, heart, and spirit.

One of my university students writes:

"Reading Fired Up Leadership (Rudnesky, 2020) and attending class have changed my life. Before my college experience, I did not expect much from myself. Now, I understand that it is because one of the five domains was undiscovered. I had no passion….. Now I do. I started believing in myself. I gained confidence. It took just one person. Believe in yourself or no one else will."

I facilitate Leadership Academies for students and educators of all ages. A sixth grader parallels the same emotion in a straightforward statement:

"Leadership made me realize the effect of small actions. I believe in myself, and I believe in my classmates."

That's a fairly bold statement from a twelve-year-old but it reinforces that the concepts of *Fired Up Leadership* are relevant to everyone.

As demonstrated in Figure 1 at the beginning of this book, all domains are continually feeding off one another. To be an effective leader, you are in all of the domains every day. As you pursue balance in life and leadership, the five domains become complementary. Balance is a key factor. You are enabled to spark change. Your passion can do just that.

Your unique talents and positive influence will get other people Fired Up! As you become more proficient, your school becomes better. Your community becomes better. The world becomes better. You and the people around you become positive change agents. Moments turn to movements. Great thinkers become great doers. You find your *EPIC!* Where your Exceptional talents meet your Passion guided by your Intelligence and Character, therein lies your EPIC.

Passion can be a game-changer and a positive disruptor. The courage to find and pursue your passion will speak volumes as you develop your mission. Some people have told me that their passion is powerful enough to be therapeutic.

> ***Your passion sets your soul on fire.***

You wake up thinking about it. You go to bed thinking about it. You start living that *Fired Up* life. Your *"WOW Factors"* and *"Magical ta-da moments"* appear every day because you create them every day.

On one return visit to our school, a student told me that he was pursuing his passion of football at the collegiate level. He was recruited to play baseball but came to the realization that his journey needed to be redirected. He played Division One football at Temple University in Philadelphia. Upon graduation from the university, he became a financial planner. He changed careers because he was drawn like a magnet to his passion of football. He became a talent scout for the National Football League.

When asked about it, he told me: *"Find the thing you can't live without and fully commit to it with everything you have. For me, that's always been football. Sometimes it won't be easy, but the feeling of knowing you're being true to yourself makes it all worth it."* After congratulating him for accepting a job with a professional football team, he said, *"Thank you, Dr. R! I'm still using all the principles you taught us over a decade ago."*

This student understood the connection that passion played in driving his leadership. He summed it up beautifully. He also fully connected his calling, career, and passion. That makes him a true gamechanger.

Name some passions you would like to pursue.

_____

_____

_____

_____

_____

_____

Some of my passions include music, magic, sports, leadership, family, friends, authoring books, public speaking. I have been blessed to follow my dreams and add to my passions.

When I was a principal, we had dozens of students that surfed and skateboarded. They were very passionate about it. One of our many service projects included collecting clean socks for the Atlantic City Rescue Mission. Our plan was to skateboard down the bike path in front of our school and collect socks. The students told me that if I skated, they would collect one thousand pairs of socks. Our engineering teacher, along with his students, built me a longboard (low and slow) and I learned. Can

you imagine? I started skateboarding when I was over fifty years old.

And behold: We collected over two thousand pairs of socks! I will never forget that experience and neither will the students. I still ride my longboard, and I get a lot of strange looks along the way but I enjoy it.

We held another skate day inside the school because of inclement weather. It was amazing! Some of the students had never attended an after-school event. WOW! A great way to think differently. It was a wonderful connector to what we do. The students thought it was the coolest thing ever to skate through the hallways. I did, too!

One of my daily goals was to walk through every classroom every day. As busy as I was on some days, just a minute sometimes made a big difference. The students and teachers were used to it. If I missed a day, or I was not in the building, they knew. When you show up every day, they expect you. If you come only once in a while, people think something is wrong when you do show up.

It was the visibility of all staffulty (staff and faculty) members that solidified a part of our culture that contributed to safety and caring. One day, I was in our engineering class. We started a conversation about the qualities of a leader. The students, teacher, and I started to come up with core words. One student had a suggestion to write them on a surfboard. Amazing idea!! We started right away!

The next time we had a group of students from another school for a Leadership Exchange, we copied surfboards on paper. Each participant wrote a leadership trait on their board. On the back, they wrote a letter to a person that possessed that quality and why. Over the years it evolved into surfboards you can wear around your neck. Just like that, Core Boards were born. After doing it hundreds of times, it really built relationships about topics that students and educators are passionate about. We even donated money to nonprofits by selling them. "*WOW! Factor.*"

Revisit the things that make you happy. Are they hobbies? Are they jobs? Are they your destiny? How will you pursue them? Write a summary of Domain Five then read it out loud and teach it to someone.

_____
_____
_____
_____
_____
_____
_____

- **Domain Five: Passion**

    - Follow your passion to lead you to your purpose
        - Develop hobbies and interests
            - Where is your happy place?
            - How do I get better?
        - Career options & opportunities
            - Career Fair
            - Internships & Shadowing

- Leave a legacy
  - What positive message do you want to leave to your school?
  - How can you leave it?
    - Legacy Wall
    - Legacy essay
    - Legacy letters

Fired Up Student Leadership Lifebook

Conclusion

An important component of leadership is growth. Because change is constant, growth must also be continual. *Fired Up Leadership* will push you to the end of your comfort zone but that is where you start to see your full potential. Other people start to see it, too. Then they become empowered by your commitment. Leadership moments turn to leadership movements, transforming your school from ordinary to *EPIC*.

As your world keeps getting bigger, so should your hopes and dreams. New places will continue to be created. Be ready. It is time to challenge some of the traditional models of education and leadership and turn them upside down. By developing a community of creativity, it allows everyone to have an optimistic future. Expand your capacity in body, mind, heart, and spirit.

> *Dream **SO BIG** that it freaks people out!*

Some people never have the courage to move away from negative environments, toxic people, or "do whatever it takes."

Too many people become average even though they are born into a wealth of opportunity. They never reach their full potential. Other people with an uneven playing field have achieved some remarkable accomplishments because they connected their life's gifts to their *EPIC.* You choose!

By the time you read this, you are well into your leadership journey. You already have more leadership training than most adults get in a lifetime, and you understand the power of your influence. Use it wisely!

About halfway through my career as a middle school principal, I had one of those common-sense moments that improved our school culture. I decided to give every student at least one leadership lesson every year and an exit interview before leaving our school. Think about how much wisdom that accumulates. We were able to fine-tune the quality of everything in our school because of this feedback.

If you want to know what a student, friend, or colleague likes or doesn't like, ask. Never underestimate the value of everyone's opinion. These opinions will allow you to modify, adjust, and perfect the excellence of your school's climate and culture.

As you fine-tune the quality of your life, you develop that "can do" attitude. Everything you need to know about leadership, you just learned. Now, you need the experiences. Make those connections to the life you are about to have. **You are enough!** Your influence carries over into the attitudes of the people around you. Keep building those relationships!

Some days my life is totally exhausting but on those days that I am exhausted, I feel growth. And any growth, I can turn into a positive outcome!

Shift happens.

Stay *"Fired Up,"* people!

Peace and love always win!

Appendix A

Fired Up Leadership Design for Students & Educators

The five domains of *Fired Up Leadership* encompass a contemporary, transformational leadership portrait that will build a leadership school by offering opportunities for all students. Each domain has key indicators that students should acquire as they move towards completion of core competencies. Proficiency in leadership and character significantly contribute to a positive school climate and culture. Schools with a positive culture notably outperform schools with disconnected stakeholders.

Fired Up Leadership

- ➢ **Domain 1 - Self-Management/Organization**
- ➢ **Domain 2 – Communication/Listening**
- ➢ **Domain 3 - Critical Thinking, Problem Solving, & Team Building**
- ➢ **Domain 4 - Character - Service Learning**
- ➢ **Domain 5 - Passion**

- **Domain One: Self-Management/Organization**
  - Practice self-care in all areas: Body, Mind, Heart, & Spirit
    - Daily hygiene
    - Schedule priorities
    - Organize your calendar/manage time
      - Be able to work independently
      - Assume responsibility
    - Keep a gratitude journal
  - Set short term and long-term goals and be able to effectively carry the plan to achieve these goals.
    - Write goals for each week and marking period
    - Write goals for each year
    - Develop a personal mission statement
  - Be able to define and understand Leadership Styles.
    - Servant Leadership
    - Transformational Leadership
    - Resultant Leadership
  - Effectively manage your attitude.

- **Domain Two: Communication/Listening**
  - Use a variety of written, oral, digital, and nonverbal communication to articulate and develop leadership skills
    - Become an effective listener through authentic listening habits
      - Practice

- Use team builders and connectors
- Improve public speaking skills
  - Infused in curriculum and/or workshops
  - Develop a digital portfolio
  - Develop competency in digital communication
    - Podcasting
    - Video - casting
  - Read out loud and make presentations to elementary schools, senior citizens, and at conferences
- Write a variety of essays
  - Infused into the curriculum using a variety of character & service topics
  - Writing prompts & free writing journal entries
- Deliver information properly and timely

➤ **Domain Three: Critical Thinking, Problem Solving, & Team Building**
  - Consider different points of view.
  - Identify, analyze, and solve problems.
    - Use a SWOT Analysis
      - Strengths
      - Weaknesses
      - Opportunities

- Threats
    - Create an action plan
  - Demonstrate teamwork skills.
    - Empower others
    - Travel with your school or other organizations
    - Learn from professionals outside of your school
    - Participate in a club, sport, band, and/or community organization
    - Complete a list of challenges
        - Participate in a Leadership Exchange with another school
            - Facilitate planning, learning, activities
            - Exchange ideas with other schools

- **Domain Four: Character and Service**

  - Demonstrate character traits.
    - Each day, week, and/or month, a different character trait and leadership quality is applied across the curriculum.
    - A variety of ideas are shared on digital media, announcements, video, and/or websites.
  - Develop Service-Learning projects and awareness.

- Read to senior citizens and/or children.
- Facilitate your own community service project – "Pay It Forward"
- Complete service at a food bank, homeless shelter, assisted living center, etc.

➢ **Domain Five: Passion**

   o Follow your passion to lead you to your purpose
     - Develop hobbies and interests
       - Where is your happy place?
       - How do I get better?
     - Career options & opportunities
       - Career Fair
       - Internships & Shadowing
     - Leave a legacy
       - What positive message do you want to leave to your school?
       - How can you leave it?
         o Legacy Wall
         o Legacy essay
         o Legacy letters

Appendix B

Inspirational & Fun Ideas from *"Fired Up Leadership"*

1. Have a yearly theme
2. Welcome forward (Happy New Year)
3. Halfway celebration
4. Roll out the red carpet (many ways)
5. Start traditions
6. Declare a service learning platform
7. Yearly staffulty picture on the first day
8. Photoshop your head on the shoulders of your favorite superhero
9. Staffulty field trip
10. Tip of the week
11. Question of the week
12. Power clap
13. Secret handshakes
14. Design, create, trade pins from each yearly theme
15. Create temporary tattoos promoting your theme and organization
16. Renaissance someone: student, staffulty, parent, community member
17. Core Boards - give one, keep one- What's your core word?
18. Pass around a beach ball and marker. Have each person write a power word on the ball.
19. The *Starfish Story* & other stories of character
20. Paint your walls with murals and quotes
21. Paint your bathrooms with quotes and murals
22. Paint your parking spaces

23. Let your students draw with chalk all around the outside of your school
24. Build a legacy
25. Leave a legacy
26. Leave a legacy and memorialize it on a tile wall
27. Name your hallways
28. Take A Number (Deli Counter Character) with inspirational quotes and actions
29. Put a candy machine in the *Staffulty Lounge* then give everyone a quarter to use it
30. Put fruit on the counter (5-star check-in)
31. Make your staffulty meeting an event
32. Have an exercise and/or yoga class
33. Spirit days
34. Have a *Leadership Summit*
35. Send a thank you note
36. Welcome people on your campus – greeter/tours
37. *Brag Board-* (hard copy and digital) Brag about your school or organization
38. Make your own inspirational posters with pictures of people you know (students and staffulty)
39. Hold up signs: *You Are Awesome! Honk If You're Happy!, Smile, etc.*
40. Invite a former student to be a keynote speaker on the first day for staffulty
41. Have popcorn paydays
42. Make breakfast for the first ten people at work
43. Buy lunch for someone you rarely see
44. Staffulty of the month

45. Create the abundance mentality
46. Have a *Leadership Exchange* (visit another school and have them reciprocate with ideas)
47. Retire a t-shirt
48. Have a secret pal week
49. Organize a pre-pep rally picnic
50. Have a *Renaissance Rally* to celebrate academic excellence, leadership, great character, and participation
51. Create a *Great News File*
52. Make positive contact
53. Have an ice cream social
54. Have A *Girls Only Day*
55. Have A *Guys Night Out*
56. *People's Choice Awards*
57. Leadership camp for incoming students (or highest grade) or any stakeholder group
58. Daddy/daughter dance
59. Mommy/son dance
60. Character commercials
61. Renaissance television (RTV)
62. Play music in the cafeteria (have people make different play lists)
63. Play music when people enter your building
64. Dance in the cafeteria during lunch
65. *"Dancing with the Staffulty"* contest
66. Renaissance stamps
67. Pass the lightsaber
68. Lip sync contest

Fired Up Student Leadership

69. Classroom makeover – for staffulty winners or surprises
70. Door decorating contest
71. *Blue/Gold Basketball Game* – students and staffulty on both teams
72. Dress Down Paydays- for staffulty rewards
73. Penny wars- for service
74. Make your yearbook an event – no one should be sitting at a desk for their picture, use your yearly theme
75. *Almost Anything Goes* (AAG) – silly and fun relays for students, parents, and staffulty
76. Pie a teacher, supervisor, or co-worker with shaving cream
77. Staffulty leadership *Relay Olympics*
78. Celebrate everyone's birthday on their door and hallway bulletin board
79. Outline the perimeter of your building with American flags to celebrate patriotism
80. *Diversity Day* -use your imagination
81. *Dear You, You Are Awesome*- inspirations that can be torn off a poster (smile, you rock, you are talented, you are beautiful, etc.)

82. Create a year in pictures and post to social media
83. Define your organization with ten pictures
84. Stand up on top of your chair or desk and yell: "I am alive!"

85. Collect smiles
86. Pass out smiles (like the free compliments)
87. Make envelopes and write on them, "open when you want to smile." Put things inside that make people smile.
88. Designate a *"Friendship Bench"*
89. Create a "come sit with me" table
90. Create a "5 star" restaurant table in the cafeteria
91. Have a guest waiter and waitress dinner
92. Fitness community night – fun and diversified
93. *Community University*
94. Barbeque hot dogs and hand them out at dismissal and to people in cars picking up people
95. Meet and greet bingo
96. Affirmation bingo
97. Diversity bingo
98. TGIM- thank goodness it's Monday
99. *High Five Friday-* with a big spongy hand
100. Icebreakers and team building activities should be a regular part of your repertoire.

For more information on these ideas to inspire your organization:
email <u>FrankRudnesky@gmail.com</u>
FiredUpLeadership.org

Appendix C

Gratitude Journal

It's simple. Every day write down what you are grateful for and how to express your gratitude. Some people draw pictures or take pictures. Be intentional. Be creative.

Create something online if it is easier to use.

Made in the USA
Middletown, DE
14 February 2025